HOW TO BE F*%#ING ANNOYING

Irritate, Exasperate, and Aggravate

LUCINDA WILDE

DOG 'n' BONE

This edition published in 2026 by Dog 'n' Bone Books
An imprint of Ryland Peters & Small Ltd
20–21 Jockey's Fields, London WC1R 4BW
www.rylandpeters.com
Email: euregulations@rylandpeters.com

First published in 2020 as *How to Be Really Annoying*

10 9 8 7 6 5 4 3 2 1

A CIP record for this book is available from the British Library. US Library of Congress CIP data has been applied for.

ISBN: 978-1-912983-95-7

Printed in China

Designer: Geoff Borin
Art director: Sally Powell
Commissioning editor: Pete Jorgensen
Head of production: Patricia Harrington
Publishing manager: Penny Craig
Publisher: Cindy Richards

The authorised representative in the EEA is
Authorised Rep Compliance Ltd.,
Ground Floor. 71 Lower Baggot Street,
Dublin, D01 P593, Ireland
www.arccompliance.com

FSC www.fsc.org
MIX
Paper | Supporting responsible forestry
FSC® C106563

Contents

INTRODUCTION

In a world full of trivial annoyances and a slow, steady drip of irritations, it can be hard to find a way to stand out. We can all be irritating without trying, but in very minor ways. To elevate your ability to annoy into an art form takes time, dedication, and attention to detail—this book will show you how.

We are told that, in order to win friends and influence people, we should smile, remember their names, make them feel valued; that it is important to be a good listener and to treat everyone with respect. In short, we should behave like man's best friend, the dog. Dogs will always greet you excitedly; they will massage your ego and hang, sycophantically, on your every word.

Some of us, however, prefer cats. A cat will give you its full attention for exactly as long as it finds you worthy of its attention. Cats are also grand masters in the game of How to Be Annoying. A cat will clear your desk in seconds, curl up in the middle of the newspaper you are trying to read, and shred your furniture. If your irritation bubbles over, they will simply stalk off. Cats do not give a ****.

There is an abundance of literature exhorting us to keep calm; to spread light and happiness. However, for those of us with low thresholds of patience and short fuses, perhaps the best way of dealing with life's constant frustrations is to become the hunter, not the hunted. Take a lesson from the cats of the world—annoy at will, then walk away.

AT WORK

Being seriously irritating at the office requires a delicate touch, because no-one wishes to end up out of a job. The best way to truly annoy at work is to appear to play the game, to show a genuine team spirit. Be the first person to volunteer for a thankless task and always be the last person to leave a meeting. In fact, meetings are an annoyance art form in their own right. Nobody has yet found a more reliable way to waste time while appearing to be hard at work than to hold meetings on every possible subject.

The further beauty of meetings is that they irritate both staff and customers. The latter are forced to leave urgent (unanswered) messages, while the members of your team with real work to do—and an appetite to do it—are trapped in the tedium of time-wasting trivia and pointless pontification.

HOLD A MEETING,
PREFERABLY ON A MONDAY MORNING.

This prolongs by an extra half day the period during which frustrated customers cannot make contact.

Ensure that every member of staff from the same department is in the meeting, so there is literally nobody at all available to answer any calls.

Make it impossible for your customers or clients to contact you by phone.

To do this, set up a series of automated messages complete with multiple-choice options that require a degree in cognitive reasoning to navigate.

Never call back.

There is almost nothing as annoying as being ignored.

Ask your customers to key in their

Account number,
Password,
Location number,
Access number,
Memorable date,
and Security code

before eventually connecting them to an operative who will ask them to repeat all of the previously entered data.

BOOBY-TRAP YOUR WEBSITE WITH CLICKBAIT OR AMAZING DISCOUNT OFFERS THAT ONLY EXIST IN A FORMAT THAT IS IMPOSSIBLE TO USE.

For example,
"75% off return flights to Tokyo (departing in one hour's time)."

BE RANDOMLY UNPUNCTUAL

It must be random; if you are always late people will allow for it.

COOK FISH IN THE SHARED WORKPLACE MICROWAVE.

★ Score extra points for fish curry. ★

LEAVE WELL-AGED, UNPASTEURIZED FRENCH CHEESE IN THE OFFICE FRIDGE,

preferably over a weekend or public holiday.

EAT THE WELL-AGED, UNPASTEURIZED FRENCH CHEESE THAT SOMEONE ELSE HAS LEFT IN THE OFFICE FRIDGE.

MASTER POLITICIAN-SPEAK,

the knack of replying without addressing any of the issues actually raised. Respond to all questions by circling back to the point you wish to make, and then repeating it.

WHEN ARRANGING MEETINGS ALWAYS SUGGEST THE LUNCH-HOUR AS YOUR PREFERRED TIME. OR 7AM. OR 7PM.

And always pick a day on which your part-time colleague is not due to be in the office.

NEVER LET YOUR COLLEAGUES FINISH A SENTENCE—SECOND-GUESS THE ENDING AND FINISH IT FOR THEM.

Make sure you get it entirely wrong.

TAKE YOUR STREAMING, HIGHLY INFECTIOUS COLD INTO MEETINGS AND THEN, HAVING SNEEZED INTO YOUR HAND, OFFER IT TO ALL ATTENDEES TO BE SHAKEN.

At a meeting, always be the person
who, when the hurdle of

"ANY OTHER BUSINESS?"

is finally reached, sticks their hand up and mutters,

"MAY I JUST ASK..."

IF WORKING IN THE SERVICE INDUSTRY, MASTER THE ART OF "WAITER-EYE."

This is the ability to make anyone trying to attract your attention completely invisible—even if their table is on fire.

SET YOUR TABLE ON FIRE.

AT HOME

If familiarity breeds contempt, then domestic life is a veritable petri dish for cultivating all kinds of irritations and resentments. Unless you are fortunate enough to be able to employ domestic help, the relentless grind of staying on top of daily chores will soon wear you down. But take heart: at least you have a captive audience and a hundred opportunities a day to be intensely annoying.

Most families enjoy a kind of ongoing low-key guerrilla warfare, where individuals deploy tactics such as extracting pungent, unwashed socks from the bedroom floor and stuffing them into the waste disposal unit, removing the plug from the never-off TV, or pointedly leaving the overflowing trash bag on the kitchen floor.

Staying cool in the face of this conflict is essential. When you are expressing legitimate rage, few things in the world are as un-calming as being told to calm down. As such, when your partner or kids finally flip, remember to smile patronizingly and tell them that on a global scale, their grievances are all very minor. For bonus points, add in a patient, long-suffering smile and a conciliatory hug.

With just a little time and thought, domestic skirmishes can be escalated into full-scale war. Just check out some of the tips overleaf.

CHANGE KEY PASSWORDS AND LOG-IN CODES TO JOINT BANK ACCOUNTS, FAMILY BROADBAND, SHARED MEMBERSHIPS, ETC.

It is crucial you do this in secrecy.

USE THE LAST OF THE TOILET PAPER, BUT LEAVE THE CARDBOARD TUBE IN THE HOLDER.

BONUS POINT:

Make sure there is no replacement roll within reach.

INSIST ON WATCHING A TV PROGRAM NOBODY ELSE IS INTERESTED IN, AND THEN SLEEP THROUGHOUT IT.

★ Score extra points for waking up every time someone tries to change the channel. ★

TAKE WOOLLEN ITEMS (WHICH HAVE BEEN CAREFULLY CLEANED ON THE "DELICATES" CYCLE) OUT OF THE WASHING MACHINE AND PUT THEM IN THE DRYER ON THE HOTTEST SETTING.

LEAVE KLEENEX IN THE POCKETS OF ALL ITEMS HEADED FOR THE WASHING MACHINE.

MAKE THINGS FOR YOUR FRIENDS AND FAMILY.

Everybody just loves filling their wardrobe with sub-par, ill-fitting, hand-knitted items that they feel morally obliged to wear occasionally.

UNDERGO THERAPY.

It may not help with your own problems, but it will supply you with a fabulous source of nerve-shredding, therapy-speak clichés with which to antagonize your friends.

"DO I DETECT HOSTILITY IN THAT?"

Call your children stupid names.

Warrior Odin Starchild and Honeyblossom Feathercloud might just be OK if you are a druid or a rock star, otherwise your kids would probably prefer you to stick to Michael and Jane.

When you finish with the computer each evening, turn off the household Wi-Fi.

Helpfully pick up the black trash bags containing the curtains destined for the dry cleaners and put them with the garbage.

LEAVE THE FAMILY CAR LOW ON OIL, OUT OF SCREENWASH, AND WITH JUST ENOUGH FUEL TO MAKE IT TO THE NEAREST FILLING STATION.

NEVER PUT CAR KEYS BACK ON THE HOOK WHERE THEY BELONG.

Instead, leave them in a jacket pocket, handbag, or kitchen drawer.

FOLLOW YOUR PARTNER AROUND THE HOUSE, TURNING ON (OR OFF) ALL HEATING OR LIGHTING THAT THEY HAVE JUST TURNED OFF (OR ON). DENY DOING IT.

★ Score a bonus point for turning off the lights while they are still in the room. ★

Boil a full kettle for a single cup of tea or coffee, then leave the teabag or coffee filter in the sink.

Stir your coffee with the sugar spoon then return it to the sugar bowl.

SLURP YOUR DRINK OF CHOICE LOUDLY AND ALWAYS FINISH EACH (AUDIBLE) GULP WITH A LONG:

"AAAAAHHHH."

CULTIVATE AN INTERESTING REPERTOIRE OF IRRITATING NOISES:

Clicking your pen

Tapping your fingers

Sucking your teeth

Sniffing

ETC.

Hog the remote and channel-surf endlessly.

When challenged, say:

"Oh, were you watching that?"

Always open a new carton of milk.

Even when there is a perfectly good one already open.

THOUGHTFULLY TIDY UP YOUR PARTNER'S* WORKPLACE FOR THEM (I.E. HIDE EVERYTHING!).

*Can also be done for work colleagues.

CHATTER IDLY TO SOMEBODY WHO IS VERY CLEARLY TRYING TO STUDY, READ, OR WRITE.

NEVER SAY WHAT YOU SHOULD SAY, WHEN YOU SHOULD SAY IT.

When others finally say it for you, look slightly peeved and mutter,

"I WAS JUST ABOUT TO SAY THAT."

MUTTER SOMETHING DARKLY UNDER YOUR BREATH AND THEN, WHEN ASKED BY YOUR IRRITATED FAMILY WHAT YOU ARE ON ABOUT, LOOK INJURED AND REPLY

"NOTHING!"

WAIT UNTIL THE LAST DISH HAS BEEN DRIED OR THE LAST SHEET HAS BEEN FOLDED BEFORE OFFERING TO HELP.

NEVER LISTEN.

Pretend to listen, half listen, listen to the parts you want to hear, but crucially always miss the key point, misunderstand the main agenda, and ask, five minutes later, exactly what you agreed to five minutes before.

SOCIAL SITUATIONS

It is said that you cannot please all of the people all of the time, but it is relatively easy to irritate most of the people most of the time. All it takes is a total lack of empathy, a complete absence of social graces, and a genuine belief in your own paramount self-importance.

For inspiration, look no further than in the upper echelons of world politics, where you will find narcissists, liars, egomaniacs, and bigots aplenty. Follow their example and you will soon be able to ruffle feathers in almost any group gathering.

Bragging, moaning, and interrupting are obvious winners, as is monopolizing the conversation or introducing subjects guaranteed to inflame, but they are not subtle techniques. Try less obvious methods, such as attempting to make everyone like you by trying too hard, being unnecessarily apologetic, or fishing for compliments. Valid multi-tasking is also a great technique; people struggle to justify their own irritation when the thing you are doing instead of giving them your full attention is clearly a good thing. "Sorry guys, I will be fully with you in less than a minute, I just have to click on this link to send another donation to the Syrian orphanage I am sponsoring."

Finally, you must always be willing to embarrass yourself for the cause of greater social unease. Everybody hates cringe!

TRY TO BE COOL.

PARENTS:

Attend parties your kids are at and dance.

★ Score a bonus point if no-one else is dancing. ★

SONS AND DAUGHTERS:

Attend events your parents are at and throw up on the carpet.

★ Score a bonus point if the event is a work function. ★

POST EMBARRASSING FAMILY PHOTOS OF YOUR KIDS ON FACEBOOK, REMEMBERING TO TAG THEIR COOL FRIENDS.

USE FACEBOOK TO SEND YOUR "THOUGHTS AND PRAYERS" TO FRIENDS IN TROUBLE, IMMEDIATELY FOLLOWED BY A PHOTO OF YOU AT A RAVE IN MAGALUF, CLEARLY HAVING THE TIME OF YOUR LIFE.

ARE YOU A LARK OR A NIGHT OWL?

Nothing is more annoying to the morning person than trying to deal with a comatose night owl at 6am, except perhaps for a night owl to realize that the entire household retired to bed at about the same time he got up.

Link your contacts to a
wide range of selected marketers
on social media and email.
Invite your friends to "like" endless
banal postings and contribute to
pointless debates.

FORGET THAT ONCE YOU HIT 30, CROP TOPS AND NUT HUGGERS STOP BEING OK TO WEAR IN PUBLIC (IF THEY EVER WERE).

Also, wander shirtless around shopping malls in the summer.

PEPPER YOUR CONVERSATIONS WITH INAPPROPRIATE FOREIGN PHRASES, AD NAUSEAM.

It helps to mispronounce them, too.

LITTER YOUR SPEECH WITH IRRITATING AND MEANINGLESS EXPRESSIONS.

Try any of the following:

In terms of blue-sky thinking

Speaking for myself

At the end of the day

Like

Basically

It is what it is.

START EVERY SENTENCE WITH THE WORD "SO".

RSVPROCRASTINATE.

When invited to an event, fail to make a decision on your attendance for as long as humanly possible and force others to put their own plans on hold while awaiting your reply.

ALWAYS TAKE A LAST-MINUTE BETTER OFFER IF IT COMES ALONG.

REMEMBER TO NAME-DROP AT EVERY OPPORTUNITY.

Develop

"MENTIONITIS."

This is when you manage to drop the name of your current obsession into every conversation, no matter how disconnected.

IRRITATE YOUR FRIENDS BY ABBREVIATING THEIR NAMES TO AN EMBARRASSING DIMINUTIVE.

Some of the best are:

Wazza for William

Lavi for Lavinia

DonDon for Donald

ADDING A "-BOO" TO THE END OF A NAME IS A WINNER TOO.

For example:

Sallyboo

Johnnyboo

Carrieboo

Offer generous financial contributions to any group activity—a holiday, cycle trip, joint party—then fail to pay up.

★ Score a bonus point if you still turn up to the event in question. ★

When meeting up with friends, show them your entire holiday photo collection, preferably as a slide-show.

CRUSADE.

It doesn't matter what subject you are rallying for/against, as long as you take crusading way too far and do it way too often.

BE A CULTURE SNOB.

Litter your conversation with references to obscure artists, quote from Flaubert and Nietzsche, and play the full cycle of Wagner's *The Ring* at family picnics.

Be an inverted snob.

Dismiss anything with any cultural value as "pretentious" or "elitist."

DRESS SO INAPPROPRIATELY THAT EVERYONE ELSE IS FORCED TO CURTAIL THEIR ACTIVITIES TO MAKE ALLOWANCES FOR YOU.

Most people agree that high heels are not ideal for walks on the beach and that some kind of hat and coat come in handy for snow-based activities.

Get one up on your Pilates-addicted or Reiki-fixated friends with casual references to your new sophrology classes.

●

How you dress can be a declaration of war.

Glamming up, knowing your son's new girlfriend will arrive wearing shorts and flip-flops, is a clear statement of superiority. Equally, dressing down when she arrives looking like a catwalk superstar makes it clear that you think she is just trying too hard.

WEDDINGS

Weddings are phenomenally annoying. First of all, just going to one is pretty irritating. Why must we congratulate the happy couple? Have they done something epic and extraordinary, or have they simply chosen a partner? Imagine if all choices were greeted with the same level of excitement.

"I'LL HAVE THE STEAK AND MY GIRLFRIEND WILL HAVE THE BURGER."

Fanfare, applause, an excited crowd gathers. Friends and family offer congratulations—or mutter under their breaths,

"IT'LL NEVER WORK," AND "I DON'T KNOW WHAT SHE SEES IN A BURGER."

Then there is the expense. For everyone. From the parents of the bride, shelling out barrel-loads of cash for a lame venue, to guests stumping up for engagement parties, new outfits, travel, a hotel, gifts, and more. Cheer up though, there are ways to retaliate.

REFUSE TO ADHERE TO THE GIFT LIST. INSTEAD, PLEAD GREEN AND PURCHASE THE HAPPY COUPLE A SHARE IN A WELL IN SOME REMOTE VILLAGE IN UZBEKISTAN. THIS ALLOWS YOU TO BATHE IN THE KIND OF SMUG SELF-RIGHTEOUSNESS THAT'S USUALLY THE PRESERVE OF BUDDHISTS OR CARBON-NEUTRAL VEGANS.

If the wedding celebrates the joining of two Buddhist carbon-neutral vegans, buy them a set of leather luggage and some steak knives.

If the happy couple drive a gas-guzzling 4x4 and eat meat like it's popcorn, buy them a carbon-offset voucher. It looks like a caring gift, but in reality it is a thinly veiled dig at their lack of environmental concern.

Make an impromptu speech three times longer than anyone can live through. Include utterly cringe-inducing stories of the bride or groom in their college years, backed by photographic or Facebook evidence.

REMAIN SOBER ENOUGH TO TAKE CLOSE-UP PHOTOS OF EVERYBODY WHO ENDS UP IN AN INCRIMINATING SITUATION. POST THEM ON SOCIAL MEDIA BEFORE THE VICTIMS' HANGOVERS HAVE EVEN HAD TIME TO KICK IN.

When the famous,

"SPEAK NOW OR FOREVER HOLD YOUR PEACE"

moment arrives,

SPEAK!

IGNORE THE DRESS CODE AND WEAR WHATEVER YOU WANT. FULL MORNING DRESS FOR A DRUID CEREMONY IN A YURT, SHORTS AND A CROP TOP FOR A HIGH SOCIETY WEDDING IN A CATHEDRAL.

Or just wear white—that should do it.

TURN UP AT THE WEDDING WITH A RECENT EX OF EITHER THE BRIDE OR GROOM.

Plan to hold your wedding on, or very near to, a major intersection/tourist destination. For added congestion, hold it on a major public holiday.

And for the happy couple themselves...

apart from actually planning a wedding in the first place, the next most annoying thing you can do is call it off at the eleventh hour. Only do so after guests' flights have been booked, gowns have been fitted, the cake has been baked, and the presents have been bought and wrapped.

FOOD

Food has become a major area of contention in recent years, which means it's time to jump on the bandwagon and become a food fascist—you will find the opportunities to be annoying are almost limitless.

For a start, when visiting friends for the weekend explain to them that you no longer eat meat, gluten, dairy, nuts, or any food beginning with B. Emphasize your point by munching your plate of freshly mown organic grass with an air of quiet superiority, while politely tolerating your companions' politically incorrect dietary choices.

Patronize everyone by telling them that you only ever buy farm-assured heritage vegetables and by correcting their pronunciation of quinoa. If you then move on to factory farming, dairy-free alternatives, prebiotics vs probiotics, and the iniquity and ubiquity of palm oil, the world is indeed your oyster.

Try visiting an establishment famous for its meat and dairy dishes. Question the waiter on the exact content of every single dish on the menu, before ordering a green salad, no dressing. Make sure everyone is aware that you are swallowing your disappointment, along with your unsatisfactory lunch.

ORDER THE ORGANIC TOFU
AND CASHEW SATAY WITH PEANUT SAUCE
AND THEN RETURN IT BECAUSE
IT CONTAINS NUTS.

INFURIATE GENUINE CELIAC DISEASE SUFFERERS BY WASHING DOWN YOUR RICE CAKE AND ALFALFA-SPROUT ROULE WITH A PINT OF BEER AND ANNOY GENUINE VEGANS BY ADDING THE MAYO DIP.

GAZE SADLY AT YOUR TAUT, WASHBOARD STOMACH AS YOU REFUSE A SECOND DRIED-BANANA CHIP, SAYING "I'D BETTER NOT."

ORDER VINTAGE CHAMPAGNE THEN SNORT IT OUT THROUGH YOUR NOSE "BECAUSE THE BUBBLES TICKLE".

CUT THE NOSE OFF THE ARTISAN BRIE OR ORGANIC STILTON ON THE CHEESEBOARD.

USE THE SPOON YOU HAVE BEEN EATING FROM TO DIP INTO THE CENTER BOWL OF CREAM.

OPEN A RESTAURANT AND PRINT YOUR MENU USING A SMALL FONT SET IN PALE-BEIGE ITALICS ON A SALMON-PINK BACKGROUND. MAKE SURE YOU HAVE VERY SUBTLE LIGHTING.

★ Bonus point if the only light is from candles. ★

Make your menu pretentiously incomprehensible, especially the prices:

Fresh Brittany oysters on Nordic rose-crushed ice with
Sicilian lemon crumb and wild micro-mint sprigs
6/36

Sustainable, basil-infused wild organic salmon's roe,
seared over locally sourced lumpwood charcoal,
with chakalaka and sun-dried goji berries
28

DOUBLE THE FINAL BILL VIA THE SMALL PRINT:

Oysters (6)	36
Salmon Roe	28
Chateau La Plonk	38
FOOD TOTAL	102
EXTRAS	
Table charge	24
Water	9
Cover charge	12
Restaurant tax	18
Booking fee	10
Service charge	25
TOTAL	200

ARRIVE AT A CAFE OR RESTAURANT TEN MINUTES BEFORE THE KITCHEN CLOSES.

Once seated, spend as long as possible examining the menu and then order the item that takes longest to prepare.

The staff will love you.

AT A RESTAURANT,
REFUSE THE FIRST TABLE OFFERED
BECAUSE IT IS TOO CLOSE TO THE DOOR.
REFUSE THE SECOND BECAUSE IT IS TOO
CLOSE TO THE KITCHEN AND THE THIRD
BECAUSE IT IS TOO CLOSE TO THE WALL.
SIT, BRIEFLY, AT A TABLE IN THE CENTER
OF THE ROOM AND THEN ASK TO BE
MOVED TO THE FIRST TABLE YOU
WERE OFFERED.

OUT AND ABOUT

As Jean-Paul Sartre wrote in his 1944 play, *No Exit*: "Hell is other people." Crowded and public places offer ample opportunities to create discord and friction, often without really trying. The simple act of stepping in front of someone as they hurry along a packed corridor or pipping them to the post for the last seat on the train is likely to result in an exasperated sigh at the very least.

The busier the place and the more pressed for time your target audience, the easier it is to achieve results. Mothers with small children are particularly vulnerable, because they are already under stress on several fronts. But beware, they may retaliate by unleashing their children. Senior citizens, on the other hand, often have time aplenty to spare and may even beat you at your own game.

Volume is a very useful tool. Discreet music or muted chatter are, at best, a minor irritation, but when you double the volume you quadruple the impact. Phone use in public places almost needs a chapter on its own.

In a bar, assume everybody is as interested in your daily life as you are. Broadcast all opinions and anecdotes loudly, preferably to someone at the far end of the bar.

Stand at the bar chattering inconsequentially to bar staff long after you have been served. Pretend to be oblivious to the crowd of thirsty people behind you.

TAKE YOUR BADLY BEHAVED, HYPERACTIVE CHILDREN AND TOTALLY UNCONTROLLABLE (LARGE) DOG TO PUBLIC PLACES AND THEN SHRUG HELPLESSLY AS THEY WREAK HAVOC.

Stare intently at your phone screen when walking in crowded places, forcing people to take extreme evasive action to avoid impact.

★ Score one point for every person you bump into. ★

Complain.

About anything.

Exude quiet superiority while finding everything slightly unsatisfactory.

RUIN THE ENTIRE SUMMER FOR EVERYONE BY REFUSING TO GO OUT WHILE WIMBLEDON AND/OR THE OLYMPICS AND/OR THE GOLF AND/OR THE WORLD CUP AND/OR THE GRAND PRIX ARE ON TV.

Drag yourself away from the sport on TV (reluctantly) and head for the beach. Next, abandon the kids and spend the whole day rushing to and from the nearest sports bar to catch the highlights.

Overstay your welcome.

Most of us know when to leave (usually when the host turns the lights off and dons PJs), but departure can be delayed for hours simply by saying, "I really must go in a minute," while pouring yourself another drink and beginning a rambling account of your latest adventure.

STOP!

It's that simple; just stop. Stop at the foot of a moving escalator, at the door of a train, in any kind of bottleneck, in front of any gate or access point, at the entrance to the metro, or in the middle of the road. This is equally effective on foot or while driving.

STAND IN THE MIDDLE OF
A PACKED ESCALATOR
IN RUSH HOUR.

•

PRESS ALL THE BUTTONS–
FLOORS 1–32–IN THE ELEVATOR
OF THE AIRPORT HOTEL.

At the cinema, talk over the end of movies, particularly at the exact point that the denouement is about to be made. Alternatively, explain the plot in detail, in advance of the movie starting.

SIT RIGHT NEXT TO PEOPLE IN NEAR-EMPTY MOVIE THEATERS OR ON TRAINS.

Prevent people from sitting next to you in full movie theaters and on trains by placing your belongings on all adjacent seats.

REAL ESTATE

In today's property market, the house or apartment we own or occupy is likely to be the biggest financial commitment we ever make, so it is little wonder that feelings on the subject can often run high.

In order to justify the mortgage that eats most of our monthly salary, we hope and trust that the property will continue to appreciate in value so that we see a return for all our outlay and effort. For those paying high rents, the very least we expect in return is to be able enjoy our space in peace.

We can create our own ambience and control our own borders. We can find sanctuary from the stresses and pressures of work and the outside world; we can nest. That is until the neighbors from hell move in next door.

For Mr. Perfect, there is nothing more galling than mowing his lawn into perfect stripes and preening his privet hedge while just over the fence the slovenly neighbors laze in their unkempt jungle, surrounded by abandoned car parts and discarded beer cans. For Mrs. Perfect, who polishes her brass and shines her glass while her family trail dust and debris through the entire house, every dropped wrapper and unwashed plate is a personal affront.

MOVE INTO A GENTEEL NEIGHBORHOOD OF WELL-MAINTAINED HOUSES AND NEAT GARDENS, THEN LET YOUR PROPERTY GO TO RACK AND RUIN.

Stick the biggest possible satellite dish on the front of your decaying house and place garish garden gnomes in your unkempt garden.

KEEP A DOG THAT BARKS.
BETTER STILL, KEEP PEACOCKS.

•

PLANT FAST-GROWING, UNRULY TREES ALONG YOUR PROPERTY'S BORDER WITH THE NEIGHBORS. NEVER TRIM THEM.

Put a hot tub in the front garden and install 500-watt speakers and flashing neon lights.

If you consider your home to be your castle, maintain it thoroughly. Drill and hammer from dawn 'til dusk; sweep fallen leaves across the border daily. Fire up your chainsaw at 8am on a Sunday.

Fail to post **WET PAINT** signs.

•

Ignore **WET PAINT** signs.

•

Paint your house cerise.

OBJECT TO ANY PLANNING PERMISSION APPLICATIONS, NO MATTER HOW TRIVIAL, AND START A "NEIGHBORHOOD GROUCH" WEBSITE ON WHICH THE SHORTCOMINGS OF ALL OTHER RESIDENTS CAN BE HIGHLIGHTED.

MOW THE LAWN WHILE YOUR PARTNER IS ENTERTAINING GUESTS IN THE GARDEN

★ Earn bonus points if the guests (or partner) have hay-fever. ★

NEVER MOW THE LAWN.

BUILD A WALL.
NO, REALLY,
BUILD A WALL!

Tell your neighbor he has to pay for it.

PAVE YOUR ENTIRE GARDEN, BOTH BACK AND FRONT, SO THAT AFTER EVERY HEAVY DOWNPOUR YOUR NEIGHBOR'S ADJACENT ROSE GARDEN DISAPPEARS UNDER SIX INCHES OF WATER.

LEAVE YOUR GARAGE EMPTY AND YOUR DRIVEWAY VACANT. PARK BOTH YOUR CARS IN THE STREET RIGHT OUTSIDE YOUR NEIGHBOR'S HOUSE.

•

PARK SIX INCHES OVER YOUR NEIGHBOR'S DRIVEWAY, THEN GO ON HOLIDAY, LEAVING YOUR CAR BEHIND.

PETS

Love 'em or hate 'em, pets are everywhere. Speak to any animal lover and they will reel off a list of the ways in which their animals enhance their lives—providing company, loyalty, and affection as well as encouraging exercise and social interaction. To most animal lovers, pets are part of the family, as beloved as their children and often as indulged. However, not everybody approves of keeping domestic animals as pets, while some actively dislike them.

Number 10's adored princess pussycat is the bird-murdering, midnight-yowling terror of the old lady at number 12, and your dog's incessant barking while you are at work may drive your upstairs neighbor to distraction. Others are genuinely afraid of dogs and find Fido's well-intentioned, over-enthusiastic welcome quite intimidating. Hygiene freaks shudder as they sit gingerly on your sofa covered in dog hair.

WHEN WALKING YOUR DOG, BE SURE TO PICK UP THE POOP, SECURELY BAG IT IN LITTLE PLASTIC BAGS, AND LEAVE IT HANGING ON TREES AND GATEPOSTS ALONG THE WAY.

After all, if left on the footpath dog mess is both annoying and unhygienic, but it will eventually wash away. Sealed in plastic and left hanging, it is a gift that goes on giving.

WAIT UNTIL YOUR MUDDY DOG HAS JUMPED ALL OVER PEOPLE INNOCENTLY OUT WALKING BEFORE ATTEMPTING TO CONTROL IT, THEN APOLOGIZE BY SAYING, "OH, HE IS ALWAYS DOING THAT!"

★ Score a bonus point if they are wearing white jeans. ★

Use talking out loud to your pet as a way of making remarks that you are too cowardly to make directly to the person they are intended for. For example,

"COME AWAY FIFI, NOT EVERYBODY LIKES DOGS OFF THE LEAD WHILE THEY LIGHT A FIRE IN THE MIDDLE OF THE CHILDREN'S PLAYGROUND."

DRESS YOUR POODLE UP AS MARIE ANTOINETTE OR ROBIN HOOD. HUMILIATE YOUR SIAMESE CAT BY MAKING IT WEAR A UNICORN-THEMED TIARA AND TUTU SET. IN FACT, JUST DRESS YOUR ANIMALS UP.

Post photos online.

BUY A HANDBAG DOG AND CARRY IT AS AN ACCESSORY. CALL IT HANDBAG.

Take your dog with you when you visit friends and allow it to jump all over their furniture, apparently blind to their attempts to discourage it.

If asked to control your animal, laugh and say,

"Oh, she's just a puppy."

Keep chickens in suburbia.

When the neighbors complain about being woken by the cockerel crowing at dawn, tell them to get double glazing.

GOING ON VACATION

Jetting away for a week should be relaxing, but almost nothing in the world is more annoying than air travel. The simple act of reaching the airport on time, parking, and finding the correct terminal can generate enough stress to ruin any trip before it begins.

If your flight has been delayed, you have to endure lengthy queues to pay five times the going rate for a coffee in the departure lounge. Waiting in line presents fabulous opportunities to annoy—wait until you finally reach the surly member of staff behind the counter. Then, and only then, ask your large, scattered group of relatives and friends what they would like. Prevaricate; be sure to discuss and argue all choices. If correctly done, this can take all the remaining time before your flight is called and prevent everyone behind you from wasting their money on airport food.

MOST DELAYED PASSENGERS WILL WAIT QUITE PATIENTLY IF KEPT INFORMED, SO IT IS ESSENTIAL TO GIVE OUT AS LITTLE INFORMATION AS POSSIBLE.

Two excellently pointless terms that convey sincerity but zero content are:

"OPERATIONAL DIFFICULTIES"

and

"FUNCTION FAILURE."

For example: "DeSade Airlines regret to announce that due to operational difficulties flight XX666 to JFK is delayed indefinitely. Please wait in the lounge for further announcements."

One hour later: "DeSade Airlines would like to apologize to the passengers who missed their flight to JFK due to the absence of any further announcements. This was caused by function failure.... We hope you enjoy your flight."

When traveling in a group, be the only one to insist on checking in luggage.

That way everybody will have to reach the airport a good hour earlier than necessary to allow you time to check in and then wait at arrivals with you for several hours while your now-lost luggage is reported.

Be the only one to refuse to pay for checked-in luggage and then ask all of your traveling companions to squeeze your excess items into their own suitcases.

SAVE ON CHECKING IN LUGGAGE BY HAVING YOUR KIDS WEAR THEIR SKI BOOTS ON THE PLANE.

This makes their ritual kicking of the seat in front of them so much more effective. If you feed them sugar and soda during the flight, their batteries will last much longer.

WAIT UNTIL YOU REACH THE FRONT OF THE LINE IN SECURITY BEFORE STARTING TO TAKE OFF YOUR JACKET/BELT/SHOES, UNPACK YOUR LIQUIDS, OR TAKE OUT YOUR LAPTOP.

★ Score bonus points for the number of times the instructions to do so were given over the tannoy while you waited. ★

Wait until the person in the aisle seat next to you has their tray down and loaded with plastic food before deciding you need to use the bathroom.

Immediately after returning to your seat, ask them to move again so that you can retrieve your plastic bag full of tiny bottles of hand cream from the overhead locker.

Walk up and down the plane looking worried.

Gaze out of the window at the wings, listen intently to the engine noise, and make notes. Talk quietly to the cabin crew, then go back to your place and check for the under-seat lifejacket.

Tilt your seat back into the lap of the passenger behind who is trying to eat their lunch. Lay back for five minutes only, then spend the rest of the flight sitting bolt upright, reading.

Never read the small print—or indeed any print—before making enquiries.

Email the owner of the property advertized as "An isolated rustic cottage set in woods a few minutes' walk from a remote hamlet" and ask, "Will I need a car?" Or, after booking a villa in Portugal, cancel using the explanation, "I have just realized that it's actually quite a long way away."

Applaud when the plane lands.

WHEN STAYING AT ANY PROPERTY OTHER THAN YOUR OWN, ALWAYS SHOWER BEFORE HITTING THE BEACH.

It will irritate your travel companions who are waiting for you to complete your perfect blow-dry before going swimming. When you return to your accommodation oiled and sanded, flop all over the furniture.

Speak to foreigners in loud, broken English—

"WE GO TO BEACH, YES?"

Remember to wave your hands at them.

AT THE BEACH, SET UP CAMP AS CLOSE AS POSSIBLE TO A COUPLE CLEARLY HOPING FOR SOME QUIET TIME TOGETHER. CONNECT SPOTIFY TO YOUR BLUETOOTH SPEAKER, ENCOURAGE YOUR CHILDREN TO PLAY VOLLEYBALL, THROW A STICK FOR THE DOG. AND REMEMBER TO LEAVE YOUR LITTER BEHIND.

FLY YOUR DRONE ALL ALONG THE COASTLINE, ESPECIALLY IF IT IS A WILDLIFE SANCTUARY AND PEOPLE ARE BIRD-WATCHING OR ADMIRING OTHER WILDLIFE.

Rush to the pool at dawn to drape your towels over as many sunbeds as possible, then go out for the day.

Leave stupidly bad reviews on social media sites.

Try "The Alpine cottage was nice enough, but it was on the side of a mountain and my kids would have preferred the beach." Or "The meal at the oyster bar was disappointing overall, because I do not much care for oysters."

ON THE ROAD

Road rage exists for a reason. In our high-pressured, time-squeezed, over-crowded lives, many of us spend our day in the car hurtling from one urgent appointment to the next. We drive to work by 9am. In our lunch break, we jump in the car to pick up the dry cleaning and some groceries, rushing back to collect the car from its parking space before our "60 minutes maximum stay" expires and we are hit with a huge fine.

Later, we leave the office on time to beat the traffic, in the hope we are not late collecting the kids from the after-school club, which would involve another fine.

Bleeding the motorist dry is a governmental art form in its own right. The moment you acquire a car you become fair game for every kind of piracy and stealth tax going—fines for speeding, fines for parking, fines for dawdling, fines for existing. Roads with lanes coned off for miles and miles, but zero sign of any work actually being carried out; pointlessly imposed 30-miles-an-hour speed limits along stretches of empty highway; out-of-synch traffic lights with resulting traffic jams.... All of these cannot fail to raise the ire and blood pressure of even the most placid driver. Is it any wonder that we become reincarnations of Genghis Khan whenever we climb behind the wheel?

At a busy fueling station, remember always to start your engine as soon as you return to your vehicle, but then spend at least five minutes rearranging your possessions, tidying your hair, applying lipstick, and fiddling with your phone before finally moving away from the pump.

BUY A 5-LITER SPORTS CAR IN YOUR 60S

(probably the only time you can afford to insure it)

AND DRIVE IN THE MIDDLE OF THE ROAD AT 30 MILES AN HOUR. WHEN YOU REACH THE ONLY STRETCH WHERE OVERTAKING WOULD BE POSSIBLE, ACCELERATE.

WHEN USING ON-STREET PARKING, ALWAYS PARK RIGHT IN THE MIDDLE OF AN EMPTY TWO-VEHICLE SPACE.

IF CYCLING WITH FRIENDS, ALWAYS CYCLE TWO ABREAST SO THAT CARS CANNOT PASS, ESPECIALLY ON NARROW LANES.

TAILGATE SOMEONE FOR SEVERAL MILES, HARASSING THEM CONSTANTLY TO PASS.

When you finally manage to overtake them,

SLOW DOWN!

WAIT AT "GIVE WAY" AND "YIELD" SIGNS UNTIL THERE IS SOMETHING TO GIVE WAY OR YIELD TO.

★ Collect a bonus point for each car in the queue that builds up behind you. ★

Gridlock your entire neighborhood by organizing a street race and closing all the roads in a 10-mile radius.

Subtly readjust your partner's seat position and mirrors every time they leave the car.

SIT IN THE PASSENGER SEAT OF YOUR FRIEND'S CAR AND WINCE VISIBLY EVERY TIME THEY PASS WITHIN A HUNDRED YARDS OF ANOTHER VEHICLE. GASP WITH ALARM AS THEY PULL OUT ONTO THE HIGHWAY AND GRAB THE DOOR HANDLE WHENEVER THEY CORNER.

Occasionally yelling

"LOOK OUT, LOOK OUT!"

is an added extra.

USE ALL THE COINS FROM THE IN-CAR PARKING STASH AND FAIL TO REPLACE THEM.

NEVER USE YOUR INDICATORS—LET OTHER ROAD-USERS GUESS WHICH WAY YOU ARE GOING TO GO NEXT.

If by edging forward slightly you can prevent a whole line of traffic from moving, do so. At any point where lanes merge, refuse to give way and stare determinedly in front of you, avoiding eye contact with the driver you are deliberately frustrating.

Use an electric scooter—on the road to annoy drivers, or on the sidewalk to annoy pedestrians.

SHOPPING

For some, shopping is more than a pursuit, it is a passion. In spite of the meteoric rise of online shopping, most weekends still see malls and supermarkets bursting at the seams with happy consumers and window shoppers.

The urge to consume drives the economy and vast sums of money are pumped into an advertising industry that coerces people into spending ever greater sums of money on things they can neither justify nor afford. Shopping addicts get high as their brain releases endorphins and dopamine, objects of desire are hunted down with dogged determination, and an average Black Friday can seem like a scene from *The Hunger Games*.

Small whiny children are dragged along by the hand and bored husbands follow with distracted expressions. In China, 77% of people surveyed say that online shopping is their favorite leisure activity, while in the UK, £29.3 billion was spent in supermarkets in the run-up to Christmas. In the western world, shopping has replaced religion as the opiate of the masses.

DEVELOP AN INTERESTING REPERTOIRE OF DELAYING TECHNIQUES FOR WHEN YOU REACH THE FRONT OF A LONG CHECKOUT LINE.

Fumbling in pockets for various money-off coupons is good; arguing the price of special offers and loading your shopping at the speed of paint drying are all valid. When you finally reach the point of payment, be sure to have misplaced your wallet. Once you have found it, pay for your entire shop in small coins.

Place a genuinely unexpected item in the bagging area, such as an aardvark, a bucket of fishing bait, or a gimp suit.

Arrive at the butcher's counter 10 minutes before closing time on Christmas Eve and ask them to de-bone your pre-ordered turkey/ beef joint/pork shoulder for you.

In the supermarket, insist that organic manuka honey is a necessity, not a luxury and that you really can taste the difference between coffee beans grown at high and low altitudes.

When shopping in company, try on three dozen pairs of shoes in 19 different stores before purchasing the first pair you tried.

Start Christmas shopping in July.

PILE 18 ITEMS ONTO THE "5 ITEMS ONLY" CHECKOUT, THEN BUSY YOURSELF WITH YOUR PHONE TO AVOID HOSTILE GAZES.

SURREPTITIOUSLY DROP INAPPROPRIATE ITEMS INTO OTHER PEOPLE'S SHOPPING TROLLEYS.

Intimate products are a good choice.

ASK THE STORE OWNER IF THE "T" IN "TURBOT" IS SILENT LIKE THE "T" IN "MERLOT."

ANNOY THE STORE MANAGER BY REACHING TO THE VERY BACK OF THE SHELVES TO SELECT THE GOODS WITH THE LONGEST SHELF LIFE, IGNORING THE PACKETS THEY HAVE PLACED AT THE FRONT TO CLEAR.

While distracted parents are busy talking on phones and blocking aisles with their trolleys, hand down chocolate bars and plastic toys to their children from out-of-reach racks.

Take your husband shopping.

RELATION-SHIPS

As Ambrose Bierce wrote,

"LOVE IS A TEMPORARY INSANITY CURABLE BY MARRIAGE."

In many cases, this proves to be true. Falling in love is the easy bit, any idiot can fall. It is maintaining the balance that requires patience, commitment, tenacity, and maturity.

"Love" is an all-purpose word, which we use for multiple different arrangements. For some it can be based on trust and compatibility or on unrealistic, dreamy romantic expectations, while for others it is all about sex, passion, and jealousy. Will our partner prove to be a great lover, a true friend, a good parent, an expert provider, a steady hand? We choose one person and expect them to fulfil all of our needs and fantasies, until death us do part. We might as well just throw all our emotional eggs into one basket and then shake hard. The fact that around 40% of US and UK marriages end in divorce shows how unrealistic this is. With such high and widely differing expectations, is it any surprise that so many of us find our significant other so annoying?

In moments of intense passion, call out

"SUSAN! OH MY GOD, SUSAN!!"

Of course, this only works if your partner is not called Susan.

THROW A SURPRISE PARTY FOR YOUR PARTNER.

Everybody loves coming home exhausted—particularly on a bad hair day when they are looking forward to a long bath and an evening on the sofa—to find a room full of glammed-up people yelling

"SURPRISE!"

CONDUCT GUERRILLA WARFARE BY "COMPLIMENTING" YOUR PARTNER PUBLICLY IN A WAY GUARANTEED TO EMBARRASS HIM OR HER.

For example, try,

"DON'T YOU THINK HER LITTLE LOVE HANDLES ARE JUST ADORABLE?"

Resolve arguments by slamming your husband's head in the freezer door. Not only will this irritate him immensely, but the freezer will probably defrost and flood the kitchen floor.

Always reply with

"WHATEVER!"

when your significant other is trying to have a meaningful conversation with you. There is no other single-word response that implies quite the same level of disrespect and disinterest.

WHEN MAKING LOVE, BE SURE TO LEAVE YOUR PHONE SET TO FULL ALERT ON THE BEDSIDE TABLE. SETTING AN ALARM IS ANOTHER OPTION.

ANSWER YOUR PARTNER'S PHONE BEFORE IT CAN GO TO VOICEMAIL AND BE SURE TO FAIL TO PASS ON ANY MESSAGE LEFT.

SNORE!

INSIST THAT YOUR PARTNER DRESSES UP FOR A SEXY DATE NIGHT IN HIGH HEELS, SHORT SKIRT, A TIGHT CORSET, AND FISHNET STOCKINGS. WHEN HE REFUSES, CALL HIM SQUARE.

DISAGREE WITH YOUR PARTNER'S PERFECTLY SOUND SUGGESTION FOR NO OTHER REASON THAN TO ARGUE. RE-PRESENT THIS SUGGESTION AS YOUR OWN THE NEXT DAY.

AGREE TO WHATEVER YOU ARE BEING ASKED TO DO, AND THEN DO THE OPPOSITE.

★ Score a bonus point for denying you are doing it, while doing it. ★

TAKE YOUR PHONE WITH YOU ON A DATE AND SPEND HALF THE EVENING RESPONDING TO TEXTS OR PHONE CALLS. REMEMBER TO THROW YOUR NEGLECTED COMPANION A RUEFUL SMILE, SAYING "NO PEACE FOR THE WICKED!"

SING ALONG OVER YOUR PARTNER'S FAVORITE SONGS, MAKING SURE TO GET THE WORDS TOTALLY WRONG.

BE ABSOLUTELY IMPERVIOUS TO ANY HINTS, NO MATTER HOW DIRECT.

In fact, when your wife remarks how pleasant it would be to have the door opened for her, barge through it first while agreeing with her.

BRAG ABOUT YOUR PREVIOUS SEXUAL CONQUESTS AND MAKE COMPARISONS.

Eye up members of the opposite sex when out with your partner and jokingly dismiss his or her complaints with

"YOU ARE CUTE WHEN YOU ARE JEALOUS."

EXPECT YOUR HUSBAND TO REMEMBER WHAT YOU TOLD HIM AN HOUR AGO.

EXPECT YOUR WIFE TO FORGET.

At the cafe, order a skinny salad while insisting to your boyfriend that you do not want fries as you are dieting.

NOW EAT HALF OF HIS PORTION.

SIGN YOURSELF AND YOUR PARTNER UP FOR A REALITY TV PROGRAM.

Preferably one involving the maximum amount of discomfort and public humiliation.

SAY, "OH, YOU CHOOSE,"
when asked to select a movie, and then react to every suggestion with,

"WE ONLY SAW THAT LAST MONTH" or **"YOU KNOW I HATE THAT ACTOR."**

When your partner returns from an outing and you are watching TV,

"OH, I DIDN'T REALIZE"

is a fabulously annoying answer to questions such as

"HONEY, WHY IS THE FREEZER DOOR OPEN?"

or

"OH LOOK, HOW LONG HAS THE CAT BEEN DEAD?"

Your response can be made even more annoying when followed by acute observations on things that matter not one jot, such as

"DID YOU NOTICE THAT BERNARD WAS WEARING A DIFFERENT WATCHSTRAP YESTERDAY?"

CHRISTMAS

Many people view Christmas with fear and loathing—the expectations, the false bonhomie, the nauseating consumerism, and the gluttony. It does, however, offer almost limitless opportunities to be annoying on an epic scale.

By November, people have divided into two, clear camps. We have the Christmas Fairies, who will be decking the halls before Halloween is even over, and the diehard Bah Humbugs, who will scowl and curse at everything festive, right up until the stroke of midnight on Christmas Eve, when they will turn into a pumpkin and be eaten by reindeer.

For those of us with art in our hearts, seeing a tree overladen with tacky lights and plastic robins is enough to send us sobbing to a darkened room. Purists prefer to rejoice next to a simple, forest-green pine silhouetted in pure white light, while others shrug in dismay at the total failure of neighbors to even light their pathway. There could even be a separate book on the heady cocktail of slow-burn irritation caused by festive family obligations and guilt trips. Being annoying at Christmas is, literally, like shooting Santa in a chimney—it is impossible to miss.

START STOCKPILING HOMEMADE FESTIVE TREATS AND TINSEL THE DAY AFTER HALLOWEEN.

(Unless you live with a family of Christmas Fairies, in which case, ban the very mention of a tree until December 24.)

Cover your entire building in gaudy, flashing, neon-lit Christmas tat by November 1

Turn on and run constantly, 24/7.

★ Score extra points if you live in a high-rise block. ★

Tell the family that in order to do your bit to save the planet and eliminate third-world poverty, there will be no electrical devices or imported gadgets for Christmas. Then spend the next day on the new iPhone you have bought for yourself.

FILL THE KIDS' STOCKINGS WITH AN APPLE, A SATSUMA, A PAIR OF HAND-KNITTED SOCKS, AND A CLOCKWORK MOUSE. WHEN THEY COMPLAIN, TELL THEM IT'S NOT MEAN, IT'S RETRO.

INSIST ON PUTTING LUNCH ON TO COOK BEFORE BREAKFAST AND DEMAND THAT THE BREAKFAST TABLE IS CLEARED BEFORE A SINGLE GIFT IS OPENED.

Agree with your family to exchange only the most token of Christmas gifts as a way of avoiding both debt and over-consumption. Next, secretly purchase and wrap lavish presents. In case this does not embarrass them (it should!), you can always leave on the price tags.

TRY GIFTING AS AN ACT OF AGGRESSION. GET YOUR OWN BACK ON YOUR SMUG BROTHER BY GIVING HIS OBNOXIOUS KIDS A SET OF DRUMS FOR CHRISTMAS.

GET YOUR OWN BACK ON YOUR PERFECT SISTER AND HER IMMACULATE HOUSE BY BUYING HER KIDS A PAINTBOX, SOME GLITTERY SLIME, AND A CHEMISTRY SET.

HIT YOUR INDOLENT HUSBAND WITH A BIG DOSE OF PASSIVE-AGGRESSIVE FESTIVE SPIRIT BY OFFERING HIM A DIY HOUSE MAINTENANCE MANUAL, A WINDOW-CLEANING SET, AND A SINK PLUNGER.

DELIGHT YOUR DIETING PARTNER WITH A SET OF BATHROOM SCALES, A BOX OF LUXURY CHOCOLATE COOKIES, AND A PASTA MAKER—ESPECIALLY IF THEY ARE ON A GLUTEN-FREE DIET.

Nothing will irritate the person who utterly loathes you more than being presented with a perfect, thoughtful gift that is beautifully wrapped and beribboned, and inscribed in perfect copperplate:

TO EDDIE, WITH ALL OUR LOVE X.

Especially when his name is Pete.

MAKE CALENDARS WITH PHOTOS OF YOU, YOUR KIDS, AND YOUR HOLIDAY.

These are ideal gifts for hostile colleagues, patronizing bosses, intrusive relatives, and sworn-but-unavoidable enemies.

★ Score extra points for every "achievement" you manage to include.★

BUY YOUR PHILISTINE FAMILY TICKETS TO THE OPERA TO BROADEN THEIR HORIZONS. AND MAKE THEM GO.

Drop out yourself at the last minute.

AND RANDOMLY...

Almost anything can be annoying and in the world of instant communication it can be shared around the world in half a heartbeat. Step outside your door with a hangover, a dodgy outfit, or a sour look, make an inappropriate remark or share an incautious joke and social media will hang you out to dry.

For some people, the girl applying her make-up on the train with complete disregard for public scrutiny makes their teeth itch. Manspreading is a red button, but then so is the guy tuned into his headphones who ignores the heavily pregnant woman with a shopping bag standing in obvious discomfort. Manners, or the lack of, maketh man.

Some voices are like nails across a blackboard, some laughs hit the nerve every time. Pointless revving of engines, pointless banging of doors, the asshole who leaves the tap running in the washroom, the chewing gum left on the seat, even the weather—especially the weather—can be infuriating. In other words, irritation can be completely random. There are opportunities everywhere, all of the time.

Carpe Diem.

Wear hats for no good reason. A ski hat is perfectly sensible on a winter walk but less so at a summer BBQ. A sombrero is annoying at any time.

Pretend to be Scottish by wearing a tartan to which you have no entitlement and saying "wee" when you mean small.

If anyone challenges you, say something vague about your great-grandfather being from the north (north London, that is).

PLAY SECRET SQUIRREL, WHERE THE RULES ARE TO BE POINTLESSLY SECRETIVE ABOUT MATTERS OF ZERO IMPORTANCE. AS IF THE FBI (AND THE WORLD IN GENERAL) ACTUALLY CARES IF YOU ATE AT McDONALD'S LAST SATURDAY.

OBSESSIVELY SHRED EVERY PIECE OF PAPER WITH YOUR NAME AND ADDRESS ON AND PADLOCK YOUR RECYCLING BOXES.

PRETEND YOU HAVE BEEN ABDUCTED BY ALIENS. PROVIDE GRAINY PHOTOGRAPHIC EVIDENCE TO SUPPORT YOUR CLAIM AND TELL TALES OF GOVERNMENT COVER-UPS.

JOIN A CULT, THE MADDER THE BETTER.

Become a hypochondriac and bore everyone with long, detailed descriptions of your ailments and symptoms. Use your infirmities as an excuse to duck out of unpleasant chores or dull social obligations.

BE DISGRACEFUL IN YOUR OLD AGE. SPEND YOUR KIDS' INHERITANCE ON HARE-BRAINED SCHEMES AND INAPPROPRIATE BEHAVIOR. DATE SOMEONE 30 YEARS YOUR JUNIOR. TAKE UP POLE DANCING.

BECOME AN INSTAGRAM INFLUENCER.

Pose for selfies outside major, iconic buildings and take limitless pictures of your food, drink, outfits, and make-up. Carry on waving your logo-plastered cocktail glass and branded handbag, while behind you Tutankhamun rises from the dead and Krakatoa erupts. Nothing disrupts your photoshoot!

NEVER TAKE RESPONSIBILITY FOR YOUR MISTAKES.

Rather than admit that you forgot to collect the dry cleaning or failed to put the trash out, invent a series of circumstances to exonerate yourself from any blame. Try...

"A VAMPIRE BAT FLEW IN THROUGH THE WINDOW, JUST AS I WAS ABOUT TO..."

or

"THE HANDLE BROKE AND I HAVE BEEN LOCKED IN THE TOILET ALL AFTERNOON."

FINALLY

A last piece of advice to help you annoy one final time.

BUY THIS BOOK FOR ALL YOUR FRIENDS AND FAMILY.

Before giving it to them, underline the things they do that irritate you most.